BE QUIET

BE QUIET

SELECTED POEMS

Kuno Raeber

TRANSLATED BY
Stuart Friebert

Tiger Bark Press * Rochester, New York * 2015

Published by Tiger Bark Press,
202 Mildorf Ave., Rochester, NY 14609.

Designed by Philip Memmer.

Kuno Raeber's picture courtesy of scaneg Verlag, Munich, Germany.

Publication of *Be Quiet,* by Kuno Raeber, translated by Stuart Friebert, made possible courtesy of Hanser Verlag, Munich, Germany.

ISBN-13: 978-0-9860445-7-1

CONTENTS

III   FROM THE HORIZON

IV   WITHOUT KNOWING WHY

V   WHO KNOWS?

INTRODUCTION

1. THE SCHOLAR, AS ARTIST, CLEARS THE TABLE

Take the plate from the table
carry it through the chambers.
Don't be confused by the dust,
the spider webs, the sawdust.
Not by the old
poison, by the bacon,
which smells in the mousetrap.

KUNO RAEBER WAS A STUDENT OF PHILOSOPHY and literature as well as a Ph.D. in History. He was also a poet, a novelist, and an essayist who took up the issues traditionally claimed by these academic disciplines and used them to produce arresting word-art. The poems in *Be Quiet* share with other good poems the capacity to penetrate and move readers, but I think they can do even more. Raeber's poems have the capacity to change readers. That's a strong assertion but as you read Stuart Friebert's close translations of Raeber's work you will find that the poems bear me out. Raeber's intellectual and emotional depth is underscored by an artistic intensity and an eye for pairing detail and issue that marks both the talented artist and the honest scholar. His poems, rich in metaphor and allegory, have an uncanny ability to communicate, or at least point at, what is just beyond direct description and rational knowledge.

In these poems Raeber not only describes the changing phases of human life, he embraces them. For him the Hero's journey is everyman's journey, but he thinks that in order to undertake it we must divest ourselves of many of our comfortable ideas. When writing about religion, war and death, he stops short of grand pronouncements, refusing to tell you which is *the cruelest month*. The enemy of both protocol and sentimentality, he is a thinking poet whose work argues that paradox is sometimes the only vessel for truth.

The book opens with "Down with It All," in which Raeber assaults our customary surroundings, our known world. "Down with.../ the/ spoons the forks the soup-/ pot and the plates down" he says, throwing everything over "the coffer-dam" until we must also get rid of ourselves: "you and me/ together and down below/ the silence…" where we are confronted by "the fish/ standing open-eyed, its/ eyes shining in the darkness/ taking us both in." Gone is our cozy sense of well-being. Like Jonah, we are overboard, under water, and we feel as if everything in our former life is open now to question. We think that even if we are not alone, what is out there "taking us…in" may not be what we expected.

2. HOW DO WE READ TRANSLATIONS?

> *if only a gust of wind*
> *tore the clouds apart*
> *or the lightning cut*
> *the swaths to pieces the lightning*
> *one minute everything*
> *significant shining one moment*
> *everything in fog*

I WONDER OFTEN ABOUT TRANSLATION, about what it really is, what can endure in a good faithful translation. What is due to differences between sentence structure, the average number of syllables in words and the import of each language's customary capitalizations, not to mention the difficulties cultural references always produce in one who has not grown up in the poet's culture? These differences, these obstacles you might say, underscore for me how much is saved in this series. Most of Friebert's translations track both the wording and the line structure in Raeber's originals. The language he has given us is sure and uncomplicated. In poem after poem we come right up against the issues and questions that surely preoccupied Raeber. It is impossible not to catch both the urgency of Raeber's inquiries and the profound attitude shifts in this extraordinary poet facing the universe in what is decidedly a one-sided collision. ("The black paper, a wind carries it into a ditch along the sidewalk,/ into the dust.../ Who can still/ grab it out of the ditch.../ A wind's/ got hold of it, dirty and torn now/ and carried, taken away.")

What Raeber needed in a translator, and what he found in Friebert is an accomplice, an eavesdropper and an articulator who can reflect both the poet's ease and unease as he wades into deeper waters. Friebert, as both ally and inquisitor, has caught on to the fact that Raeber acts as servant to the timeless and universal. It does not matter if the poem's setting is a barn, the ocean, or a room where a piano student practices. The grounding for each poem is the reader's center and the time is always now. Reading the translations we still feel the tenacious hold of crucial questions that haunted Raeber as he focused on both our circumstances and our limitations. The manuscript's ordering suggests that it is just as we approach answers or the understanding that there are no answers, that life swallows us up ("The last of the ballast thrown/ over and the gorges/ blue./ The dizziness./ The sun hot./ Hotter./ Snow-white.")

3. LEARNING THE LANGUAGE

In the void a word
like a white
tomb in the sand
like a bird on a
stone without a legend.

LIKE CELAN OR VALENTINE OR RILKE, Raeber could never be described as an "easy read." This is not because the poems' imagery is not intense and enthralling ("The parachutists/ roll around in the topsy-turvy winds and/

only turn sober/ on the ground"), nor that the issues the poems are built on are not gripping ("Can't you wait till/ the grave caves over you,/ why are you knocking, why crying?"). It is because Raeber's poems never explain themselves. They speak quite plainly really, and don't worry about being accessible. They ask us to read with our minds in gear so that we may do more than rely on what has been received. For the poem to live fully as we read it, we must in some way contribute. ("A boat without sails a tree/ turned in on itself and motionless on one/ shore. The other way/ on the other side of the water/ invisible.") Although the world we live in today is not the same as the one that Raeber inhabited, we too find ourselves alive and coming to some kind of consciousness within belief systems that require examination. We too are facing whatever is on the other side and invisible. In a poem titled "Fjord" he writes, "Between the narrow/ walls feather flurries. The ship/ in the depths. Feathers/ on the deck and/ drops of blood./ War in the heights." That's all. But don't you find you have to think about that?

As you read the poems you will find it increasingly easy to enter into the heart of the work. Just as your reading of Celan or Valentine is enriched as you become more familiar with their imagery and obsessions, the reader of *Be Quiet* begins to get a feel for Raeber's poetic vocabulary and his deepest concerns. That knowledge becomes a powerful resource and allows the later poems to be read more fully. That's why I find it remarkable that the ordering of the poems in this book is not Raeber's but Friebert's. The arrangement seems inspired and even inevitable, perhaps because Friebert is particularly well-qualified to do this work. Although he is a native speaker of English, he is so at home in German that he has published four books of poems in that language. He not only knew Raeber, he communicated with him for years. Friebert's extensive experience in translation (see his translations of Günter Eich and others as well as his co-editorship of the Field Translation Series), his immersion in German culture and his close reading of these poems make him an inspired guide. Reading *Be Quiet* front to back I was reminded of the precision and elegance of a yoga practice in which the beginning postures, while worthwhile on their own, prepare the student for later more difficult postures.

Weeds of Forgetting, the final poem in the book, certainly has a special power when read in the light of the previous poems.

4. THE POET INVITES COLLABORATION

> *Rest on no armchair, it'll break,*
> *its feathers sticking you in the butt.*
> *Keep going through the rooms, don't*
> *spill the soup; not till you reach the end,*
> *where the portraits of the dead...*
> *...hang below*
> *panes covered by dust, there, in the last*
> *chamber, put the plate down in the ashes: eat!*

RAEBER HAD A LOT OF CONFIDENCE in his readers. In *Be Quiet* he is always asking us to join in, to offer an opinion or tell our own version of the story. It's as if invoking the archetypal and the everyday, together we can bring something to life. In *Miracula Sti. Marci II Cure of a Sick Physician and Rescue of a Ship in the Same Night* he asks "Night traveler, where do/ you want to get across to?" That's a question that could open our reading of many of these poems. We need to read them in light of our journeys. We need to invest in and actively respond to them. In much the same way Anglo-Saxon riddles do, Raeber's poems often sketch moments that we feel a need to interpret and complete: "Twilight and a breeze/ from the meadows. The path/ a snake alone/ into the unknown and white." Involving ourselves with Raeber in this project of expanding the poem's meaning we create the truth-teller's paradox—that what we have most in common is the solitary nature of many of our deepest experiences and most significant insights.

A number of Raeber's poems use symbols which are also used by sects of the Christian religion (fish, snakes, potsherd, shepherds, Egypt, David and Goliath). Quite naturally, those familiar with and devoted to those faiths read these poems as if Raeber meant those as Christian references, and perhaps he did. Interestingly, however, most of the poems work as well, and speak as powerfully, if the references are experienced simply as ancient powerful imagery now grown into a central part of the human story. Raeber was so thoroughly at home in the world of nature and symbols that he accessed not just the symbol as appropriated by dogmas, but the very reasons they became "symbolic" in both religion and literature. Consider "Barefoot bareheaded the world/ left behind the butterfly caught in/ the cave…" There are, of course, religious interpretations of butterflies as transformative and of caves as repositories of texts and even as the tomb of Christ, but Raeber by pairing these images gets at why the butterfly became such a symbol of both miraculous spiritual growth and incredible vulnerability, i.e., why it is capable of carrying a reference to transformation forgotten and imprisoned in a cave. He seems at home in both the world of Christian iconography and the more ancient myths and stories. Thus in the third section of *Be Quiet* we find poems with titles like "Tree," "Stone," "Plank" but also poems about St. Sebastian, John the Baptist and the miracles attributed to Saint Mark.

4. THE ARTIST AS MUSIC-MAKER

The drone shatters the pane,
the shadow buries you. Shining from the sill,
smoothing its feathers, yellow and
trembling and singing
a tiny bird.

WITH RAEBER SOME HARD THINKING IS REQUIRED, some active interpretation is necessary, and that's fine. But the poems also invite us to a pleasurable passivity, a rolling in the waves of their music with stern moments and moments of delight. In this way the poems work on you, changing you the way any sweet discipline will. They will work on you like this:

Last night the snow started to melt. I'm sitting
here in the gutter, cars
are spraying me. People
are driving home from the theater. And
from the tree a cicada's flying my way,
which no one else has seen,
down into my open hand and
sings as long as I want.

The theater's long been closed. I'm sitting
in the gutter and holding
my hand outstretched, it's not
tiring: my cicada's
singing.

—Deborah Bogen

I

CLOSE AND CLOSER

DOWN WITH IT ALL

Down with it all
all of it over the coffer-dam
down with the
spoons the forks the soup-
pot and the plates down,
down with it all the dolls the
bears the train and the
stuffed elephant
down with the
pants the jacket the shoes
all of it all of it
over the coffer-dam down with
the chairs the tables the
beds all of it
all of it down and into the
sudden fall of the water
down and at the end
down with you and me right behind:
as in together as in
over you and me
together and down below
the silence the silence the fish
standing open-eyed, its
eyes shining in the darkness
taking us both in.

STILL LIFE

And the cracked egg the
burning house and the taxi
with the body in the back seat the
snails on its
forehead and cheek
on the jetty the ribs
of the ship on the beach the
dead birds smeared
black the bones
in the crystal coffin
mounted in gold and pearls
crowned with rubies the flowers
yellow the broom and the
ladyslipper purple the smoke
from the chimneys bent
over the roofs the dog dead
in the hole in the ground the locomotive
rusting on the overgrown tracks the angel
with the drawn
sword on the top
of the tomb the ripped
open chest the heart
aflame the wind
hard and sandy coming from the
dunes the flowers
monkshood and dragon's comb buried
under thistles the bursting
stalks and out of the
cloudcuff
the hand with the rose

THE PLATE

Take the plate from the table,
carry it through the chambers.
Don't be confused by the dust,
the spider webs, the sawdust.
Not by the old
poison, by the bacon,
which smells in the mousetraps.

Rest on no armchair, it'll break,
its feathers sticking you in the butt.
Keep going through the rooms, don't
spill the soup; not till you reach the end,
where the portraits of the dead
czar and czarina, almost
unrecognizable by now, hang below
panes covered by dust, there, in the last
chamber, put the plate down in the ashes: eat!

SPLASHES

The splashes on the
mirror the crumbs
on the eaten-off
table no
message the
bones in the pail
not even a
threat in the half-
open window four
months now of winter the
canal in the fog
in the pool
covered with ice no message and
definitely no threat the foot
not even set on the first
step the
suction in the cellar and an-
nounced by beetles
but black and shining
the leather of the seat in the
creaking elevator and on the
mirror the splashes

PRISON

Coming from the dull
mirror—a rill.
Sluggishly.
Closer and closer.

GLADE

The glade again
overgrown silted up
the pond no
posts no footbridge no moon anymore
sickle-shaped right
in the middle of the wound.

ILLUSIONS

The shimmer of beetles. The white
parasols hovering
extravagance of flowers. Whispers
of memories. The hour
between three and four in the morning.
And winter more than ever
an illusion.

MYSTERY

Or up there on the
white surface over
the rising water
if only a gust of wind
tore the clouds the clouds apart
or the lightning cut
the swaths to pieces the lightning
one minute everything
significant shining one moment
everything in fog
or up there who knows on the white
surface or over the rising
water who knows?

SUMMER AND WINTER

Summer inside and inside
sleep on the skiff.
Winter outside and always
in winter waking up outside.

ICY NIGHT

Because they're already beginning to set the chairs
on the table at ten o'clock,
you drive along through the night
shot through with crackling ice and find
a pub still open in the most ordinary neighborhood,
where an old man in the corner's
neatly piling up coins.
But now he's turning the radio louder
so your hard-edged thoughts sink down
into the whipped cream of pop songs.
And when you glide along drunkenly
in your latest escape and hit the ice,
you keep going right on through Greenland
and Siberia with your cheeks cut by splinters
from the windshield:
your blood melts the North Pole,
and your eyes spark behind it,
hot pebbles in the sand.
After fevering along from wine bar
to wine bar in the icy night,
your cheek, shrinking from any
grazing glance, comes to rest
on Ostia's sea-cheek.

LODGINGS

Lodgings white
little playthings of insanity.
The flood rising. In the windows
the wind. Torture
without mercy.

STREAM 1

The fishermen.
The skiff.
The fish like lightning.
The headstone in the stream
mirrored, enormous.

STREAM 2

A boat without sails a tree
turned in on itself and motionless on one
shore. The other way
on the other side of the water
invisible.

THE FISH AND POSEIDON GONE UNDER

The fishmonger empties
her pail out onto the street: the water
doesn't collect against the hot
asphalt and evaporates even
before it realizes it.

But the fish had gotten
far enough to be caught
early this morning:
"Ever since I pushed up
into the light and the warmth,
from which a long time ago the top
fish plunged back down,
starfish in its ear, polyps on its pectorals,
and now lies on the bottom:

Ever since I shot up
I've been afraid: the coolness
wasn't there anymore. My gills
grew stiff. My fins
found no resistance anymore
to be able to move ahead...

Are we all headed there, to lose
like the top fish gills and fins?
Top fish was an exaggeration. You
have to remain below and avoid
the suspicious heights.
From tomorrow forward I want
to dwell in his one still free
ear, where memory's at once
incentive and admonition..."

That's as far as the fish got
before getting caught this morning.
But the water the tradeswoman pours out
won't rise up from the hot
asphalt and evaporates even
before it realizes it.

ORPHEUS IN THE HARBOR

There's nothing here
that you'd absolutely have to have seen:
I don't like it here for the monuments:
but because of the hours
where you're deeper in Venice
than even on the Rialto:

On the hostel's hill,
your ear sharpened to the tune of stars
ringing over the harbor—
even if too far off, so the cold cries
of the blowtorches from the docks over the water
wouldn't sharpen and grow.

Don't cling to my arm:
don't be afraid
when you see the huge face white between the ships,
its mouth open,
gone dumb and as if asleep.
Don't be afraid, because a secret
stream floated it toward you even in this remote harbor:

you may ever flee cities and harbors,
I think it'll always find you again.
So look past it, and just climb the hill:

from there it's simply only the moon,
modestly with stars, if you only wish it,
lying there among the ships in the basin:
don't be afraid.

ANGELS IN THE RAIN

Angels in the rain,
miserable, with wet
wings, moving
barely over the ridges. Till one,
April, finds
a sunny spot, feathers
foaming up, and limbs
rowing, suddenly dried out, he circles
down, giant insect.
Angels with wet
wings moving in the rain.

THE DAM

The birds' feathers are stuck together.
They're sitting rigid on the oily water.
Hurry, because you don't know
when the oily water will overspill the dam.
Sing, because you don't know when your voice
will sink down in the cries of the birds,
when the dam, when your voice drops down
into the oily water, on out to the tankers.

VOID

In the void a word
like a white
tomb in the sand
like a bird on a
stone without a legend.

II

AND FAR BELOW

IF IT CAME

If it came
if it came once
again across the pond the mast
righted anonymously
at the bow and the black
sheet at the stern
the scaffold and the huge
bell the beams
groaning if it kept
coming once more as if
no one budged it
and under the dropping
stones kept
coming and heading toward
the breach and moving out through
the hole this time and spent itself
in the white in the wide
thrown open jaws way
out there this time

THE SCAFFOLDING

The builders
have spread spiders into
the scaffolding. They turn
hard as stone in the mistral and rattle.
Earlier great
brocaded curtains hung everywhere
from the beams.
But they melted
in the heat. In the evening
there were red puddles, and people
thought a murder had happened.
A few leftover threads
fluttered in the mistral.

BEYOND

Beyond the blackish
bogs behind the arid
thickets the wide
pebbly stretch on the beach
beyond the windswept
slopes with the barracks
beyond the gullies full of
skeletons beyond the leaky
boats of storms of ship-
wrecks of miracu-
lous rescues beyond
beyond the warm
gulfs of enchanted
islands beyond the outermost
fringe and the last of the very
last moment
beyond

GRAVE

Over the grave the bird will
set one white
crying-stone upon another.
The woman buried won't
see the column of cries upon which
the bird settles
at last and spreads its wings
out stiffly so that
the winds do skim but
never shift them.

JOURNEY

The head into the water. And then
the woods right up to the beach. The flat
sleepy waves. And in the treetops the vivid
cries of birds.

The head out of the water. And then
just the same pool again. In the spindly
reeds the chattering
of the duck. The beach the waves
the treetops the vivid
cries forgotten.
But the head

BEACH

Dead the bird
on the water and black. And black
and dead the dog on the beach.
But the cliffs at the rim
silvery in the evening. In the evening
dead the last shot
of wisdom in the water and dead
wisdom's last upshot
and black on the beach.
But silvery at the rim.

THE DEAD BIRD

Spring full of wings and the scattered
spring leaves lie under the black
ant-snow of their winter,
which would also melt this flat image
—formed quickly by the car's fall wheels
from the stuff and color of the patterns—
on the ground: if the boy's gaze-net
cast out from the edge of the road
didn't pull it into the pond
of his eyes, still blinking from
his lips smacking, his apple-chewing mouth:
far off from the dream and the stormy
summer, casting up the image from
the ground, where it's long been, rocking
back and forth on the surface and finally
sinking down, only to be eddied back up
again later, blunt and black.

BEACH SKETCH

On the beach the cadaver
left by the water. The vulture
on the cliff.
More and more awake
with the rising heat. Anticipating
noon. Anticipating the crisp
ready victuals.

SEA CRAB

From the edge of the pool
if it saw the blue
sail out there over the blue
sea under the blue
sky what would
the crab do
about the three blues?

But the bottom
of the pool the way back
can't be dodged.

FERRY

You're punching holes with
the oar into the metal, whose edges
will soon rust. The swimmers
will drown. The feet of the traveler
have sunk in the sand. Your glance
pins him down. When you arrive
and pull him out with
your hand it's too late.
He recognizes your face
under your hat.

COURSE OF THE WORLD

If I came right at you and
knocked you down and
stamped on you and
crushed you and scattered
the dust to all winds:
scarcely I'd raised my head again, look,
you'd be standing there again huge
and on your lips the quiet
suggestion of
an amused smile.

CICADA

One day just my voice
will be all that remains of me.
You'll look for me in
all your rooms,
on the stairs, in the long
hallways, in the gardens,
you'll look for me in the cellar,
you'll look for me under the steps.
One day you'll look for me.
And everywhere you'll just hear
my voice, my high monotone
singing voice. Everywhere
it'll meet you, everywhere
it'll fool with you, in all
rooms, on the stairs, in the long
hallways, in the gardens, the cellar,
under the steps. One day
you'll look for me. One day
my voice will be all that remains.

HORSES

Below in the cellar of the tower
the horses are going round and round.
They're pumping water, it's running
from the rocking pipe-opening. We're sitting
in the room, we're talking
and drinking one beer after another,
we're smoking cigarettes quickly.

Below in the cellar of the tower
the horses are going round and round.
The water's plunging, a cataract,
from the wobbling pipe-opening.
We're losing our way in the room, holding
ourselves to the walls, whispering, the beer's
spilled. We're smoking our last cigarette
with quick drags. The moon's
swimming off, so the pipe won't
tear it open.

Below in the cellar the horses
are racing around and sweating.

THE GUTTER

Last night the snow started to melt. I'm sitting
here in the gutter, cars
are spraying me. People
are driving home from the theater. And
from the tree a cicada's flying my way,
which no one else has seen,
down into my open hand and
sings as long as I want.

The theater's long been closed. I'm sitting
in the gutter and holding
my hand outstretched, it's not
tiring: my cicada's
singing.

MOUNTAIN CLIMB

And through the woods
on up and through the meadows
on up and through the scree
on up and then the top
and then the snow
and then the icy wind and far below
in the depths the sea
frozen, old as stone.

BUT OUT INTO

But having gone out
into the water
and farther and after the
pebbles the sand
and farther
out the mud and
farther and deeper
your feet giving way out there and no
sounds of crunching anymore and no
clinking just more
gurgling again
and again the same
vague thoughts.

UNCHANGED CHANGED

Unchanged the woods the ponds.
Unchanged the swimming roses.
The swimming roses
the ponds
the woods
unchanged.
Changed.

III

FROM THE HORIZON

GROTTO IN THE EAR

And in the grotto the thunder
of the wave in the ear
the coffin of gold in the grotto
in the ear the thunder of the wave
in the ear in the grotto
the coffin in the wave
in the ear.

TREE

The huge tree. The crown
black with
leafy lodgings. But later, birds
frozen in the empty branches. The flight
to Egypt a failure.

STONES

Lying there, veined,
stones from the depleted
pits. Seam of pavement.
Seam of a depleted Egypt.

You're traveling in the evening
as always by coach along
the promenade to the sea.
But the morning clatter of pails and sweeping
brooms on the stones no longer wake you.

The desert came over the gardens,
stunned the stones, seam
of pavement, seam of a depleted Egypt,
echo of hoof-beats from the walls. Stones
lying below would be veined. They're lying
there for you, stunned once more,
in an Egypt depleted, its pits all filled up.

PLANK

Whoever climbs along
the pyramid's plank recognizes
the missing city and sees
the dead man sitting in the ferns.
Whoever climbs along
the pyramid's plank will jump
down among the ferns and take
the cat from the dead man's knees.

UNDER THE GRATE

You're cowering under the grate,
you can't defend yourself, when David
runs across it with dirty
feet, when Goliath's head
tumbles down from sticky fingers.
When Goliath's blood
drips onto your face,
you can't defend yourself.
All bent up, you're cowering under
the grate, you can't defend yourself.

ACROSS THE STEPPE

The forgotten king moves across the steppe,
while his wagon
turns and whirls up
a veil. Between his teeth,
the bewildered, forgotten king chews nut kernels
given to him by a guard.
After a breather
the forgotten king moves on, hesitating
because his train's
caught in the thistles. He chews
the kernels of the last
nuts between his teeth and keeps going,
while his wagon
turns, disappears, his train
between thistles, the king
bewildered, forgotten.

NURSING

Without the crown and w
the veil and without the
damask gown.
Without the chemise.
The brimming breast.
The nipples
between the lips.

THE DUST CLOUD

Are the Persian horsemen out there
throwing that cloud up on the horizon?

If they flew this way they'd
surely be disappointed:
because they wouldn't find the Emperor
in his purple tent, they'd just find
the unshaven traveler, no guardian
angel, his face veiled, would turn away from.

Guardian angels disguise themselves and only
turn around in purple tents.
But the air's long
leaked out of the tires.
And even if a lance
shot out of the cloud,
it'd cut through a rusty radiator.
And if the army's ranks nonetheless
fell apart, then only so they'd
collect around the car to see: the make,
the year, the number of horsepower.

But likely nobody hurls lances anymore,
undoubtedly they all have seen newer
cars and ride past in panzers...

Are the Persian horsemen,

the guardian angel and the purple tent,

are they Julian's,

are they his very own death that the cloud over

there's been dragging toward him from the horizon?

PUNIC WAR

One
behind the other and deep
in the fog the
low hills and then the
fluttering above in the
rain the
fluttering in the snow yet right around the
next curve the high
piles by the water the many
galleys one
behind the other the entrance
blocked captured
elephants outside their
raging trunks and around the
next curve again
the hills the fog
again the fluttering
in the rain in the snow in all
walls the holes jolted
by the sound of the trumpets.

THE ENGELSBURG:
THE EMPEROR HADRIAN SPEAKS

When I opened my eyes in the chamber,
I became frightened and began
to feel my way up through the tomb.
Up above I arranged my rooms,
where I went about in heavy brocade and,
full of desire for overdoing it, wore a triple crown:
the remains of modesty,
which I still bore in life from the ancients,
I abandoned altogether now,
because my soul's arc had since become so important.
And only occasionally, to relax,
I applied myself to language and the gestures
of ecstatic fish,
which without reflection simply
swim along quietly ashimmer.
Till I finally,
after many attempts
of trying to portray my imperium,
so that none, whom it seized,
could ever free themselves again:
decided on one of the images,
which have long been effective, even after they
draw suspicion of pure masquerade to themselves,
and stepped out on the battlement:
wings still spread from flying down,
sticking the plague's sword back in the sheath,
in short, in the pose
of the angel appeasing the city from these heights,

reconciled, after a lengthy grudge, finally pacified
by pleas, ashes of penance, candles and processions,
and hence piously held in memory.

INVENTIO ET TRANSLATIO CAPITIS
STI. JOHANNIS BAPTISTAE

I rub my eyes in the morning.
But the driver
sees the skull without dread
in the trunk behind the cannisters.
Who'll bring it secretly inside now, so no one
sees it, before it's exhibited on the altar in Constantinople?

The driver takes the skull
from the trunk and wraps
it in a blanket on the seat and drives
off without dread and on to Constantinople.
I'm standing here wide awake in the morning.

PETER PAUL RUBENS: SAINT SEBASTIAN

Whoever'd be able
to lead you out to the reedy square,
where the old man with the muddy beard stopped
a moment while emptying his pitcher of river water,
in order to discover, if in vain,
why you're standing there moaning by the tree:

whoever'd be able,
may he be spared convulsing
in the lapis lazuli cave of the church
from the whirring of every single arrow
striking your body
from the ambush of prayers.

Outside the angels would swing
down from the branches to dry up
your blood with linen,
so the old man's astonishment would be even more mute.
If with some effort he finally might recognize you,
the airy spirits, river women, dryads, thrust aside, scarcely would:

Whoever'd be able...

MIRACULA STI. MARCI II
CURE OF A SICK PERSON AND RESCUE
OF A SHIP IN THE SAME NIGHT

Night traveler, where do
you want to get across to?

At the edge of the moor's sleep
I flee past to the firmer
water: just now a ship's
stranded on the reef and calling me.

So quickly give me your hand,
night traveler, out into the moor's
sleep: give me your hand!

He touches me just with his finger, moving
quickly across the sea. Yet here I sit
cured in the morning, which travels
quickly. And the ship
sails right in, which the fleeing traveler
pulled off the reef with his finger and, a toy now,
thrust right into the cry of
the children running toward it.

MIRACULA STI. MARCI III
THE LOST CORPSE

The lagoon stinks:
Each slap of a wave washes
muck onto the steps of Santa Maria della Salute.
The old woman in the motorboat holds
her nose. But she's happy the palaces
are starting to collapse.
So perhaps they'll find the body
of Saint Mark again.
The canons who preserved him
have all died. They had no
money for new ones, to whom
they might have passed on their secret.

The jobless on the crumbling bridges
don't dare look at one another and fish
for food tins. There are a lot
from the old days, when strangers still
came this way. In the meantime it's likely
the body of Saint Mark went lost. And everyone
fears death in the swill, which is gradually
beginning to congeal. The lagoon
stinks.

MIRACULA STI. MARCI IV

The pigeons
rise up from the square
and coo and are surprised,
wings awhirr, that
someone who doesn't even have wings
doesn't stay on the square to feed them.
Why he climbs on the scaffolding and builds
towers.

They can't imagine that for masons
towers are worth building, stepping
amiss, plunging. The hand of St. Mark,
walker-on-air, takes them by the crest,
and lays them gently out on the beam.

The crest hurts for a long time afterward.
And the pigeons
coo and remain surprised, wings awhirr.
They don't see the air-walker, Saint Mark.
The mason doesn't see him either. But
he keeps to the beam, terrified
and happy: the top of his head hurts.

MIRACULA STI. MARCI V

A stone strikes the mirror. You see yourself,
winged lion, in the mirror.
It breaks, and the hangman
bores the wood into your eyes.
It splinters. He wants
to cut your wings off. The iron
melts. You won't need to
return to Venice. You're still
the winged lion.

A stone strikes the mirror.
But the iron, the wood
recognize you anyway.
Venice is only a mirror.
The column's tall.
The waters don't reach your eyes,
don't reach your wings.
Don't be frightened, look at yourself,
winged lion, in the mirror.
A stone strikes the mirror.

MIRACULA STI. MARCI VI
THE CORPSE IS FOUND

The motor's quiet now.
Swinging and shouts
from the footbridge: they've found him!
Swinging and shouts, stench of fish, the yellow
corpse. The church
is lit up and full of smoke.

The motor starts, and I flee
from the shouts and the stench
of the fish, the yellow
corpse, vomit
over the railing and taste,
anew and sober, the sea in the outer lagoon.

MIRACULA STI. MARCI IX

Nobody pulls the one sitting there
from the boat before it sinks
unless it's Saint Mark.

Whoever's entreaty pulled him from
the cloud of storms the mighty illusion,
also took hold of his luminous hand
and climbed over and left
his votive image on the pier's pillar.

The boat
can't understand now and rouses
the waves and strikes the pillar till it falls.
The body lying behind is dessicated.
Its hand
holds nobody now, everyone drowns.

Because nobody pulls the one sitting there
from the boat before drowning,
unless it's Saint Mark.

IV

WITHOUT KNOWING WHY

GARDENS

Gardens in your sleep
stirred by noises.
Hum of grasses scent
of black bumble bees. The thunder
still faint and down below
the menace.

BEES

Not much longer, not much
will you twitch from the sound
of your steps in the stony hall.
Not much longer, not much till you step
into the bees in the corner of the stony hall.
In your ears droning,
in your nose the odor
furtive and long and angry
in the corner of the stony hall
of collected honey.
Stings.
Not much longer, not much.

BEETLES

A few beetles vivify
the leaves, freezing in the light
of the lamp; it's bobbing
this way over the water. Your fingers
trembling suffice, and the leaves
turn, die:
be quiet!

ABANDONING BUTTERFLIES

—for Karl Rössing

Barefoot bareheaded the world
left behind the butterfly caught in
the cave and the
noise of the pieces
barefoot bareheaded the world
left behind the delicate
butterfly but
shut in but
caught and the
noise of the pieces
barefoot bareheaded the world
left behind and shut
in and caught
in the cave barricaded
the dark the delicate
butterfly
abandoned abandoned.

THE ARROW

The arrow whizzes
and travels along the boulevard
and stops on the island in the crown
of the red plane tree.

The whizzing, the rope
pulls the bus along the boulevard
across the bridge to the island:
I'm looking for the arrow
in the crown of the red plane tree.

The other trees are still
all green. And the kites
slowly reach them
and hang
inert in the branches.

My arrow in the red
plane tree is dead.
The bus travelled too slowly.

FJORD

Between the narrow
walls feather flurries. The ship
in the depths. Feathers
on the deck and
drops of blood.
War in the heights.

RIVER HARBOR

If they saw how the Spanish flag's the last to flutter along the dockwall,
would the women still take some cake with their tea and the hunchback
still read his magazine, his stiff hat next to him on the ledge?

As if the ships hadn't already begun to carry the city into the sea:
and only as long as there's loud hammering to drown out the gossip and bustle,
in order to finish the last ship, is there time
for cake and tea and turning pages in magazines.

Yet if they saw the Spanish flag as the last to flutter along the dockwall,
they'd quickly prepare for departure, like your eyes that have left me
and are swimming along the dockwall in the middle field of the Spanish flag.

ISLAND

Bells pealing. An old
island. And no
airfield no harbor.
But nearby but nearby.

AIRPLANE

The drone shatters the pane,
the shadow buries you. Shining from the sill,
smoothing its feathers, yellow and
trembling and singing
a tiny bird.

HELICOPTERS

Black barracks
stand in the clearings.
The helicopters dive and put out
the light. The inhabitants
take off for the karst,
where rosemary grows and where
the sea's shroud lies
way down below.
The helicopters scratch away,
but they can't lift it.
They hum
unobserved in the sky,
although like swarms of midges
they sink and climb.

WINI

Under the
foaming
The win
Shadow
tents. In
the stil

ARACHUTISTS

The parachutists
roll around in the topsy-turvy winds and
only turn sober
on the ground. The boats
are leaking, and the islands' inhabitants
don't miss knowing
how to build boats anymore.

The parachutists
bring their white
tents. Set up,
they smell of spices, which priests
mix for the Feast
of Fallen Angels. Down
on the ground, they're
no longer sober anymore. Odor
of spices, drums, drums, trampling.

MOMENT/Blink of an Eye

From the table, where she was praising the airplane
to her friends, which brought her from Detroit
—it's in Michigan, a land in the States like Swabia in Germany—
to show her children, Barbara and Christofer,
to her parents,
she looked over at him, moving her eyes, quickly
moving her head and her hand with the rings,
still the same way she always did, when he
talked down at her that August
from the hammock in the garden,
which she playfully pushed at from below;
but only spoke so she'd
throw open her dark roving eyes at him
and move her head and quick hand without rings.
The way she opened them now, going on
about Detroit and the airplane to Swabia
and did not acknowledge him:
who got up and, stricken, almost forgot to pay,
because he no longer could bear looking back
at the swaying garden hammock that night in August.

FALL DOWN LIGHTLY...

fall down lightly,
; you think you've
it in your hand. Then it's
ttlecock, which two children
ying with. It's a tin
with the stinking remains of sardines. You run
along the houses, from which a tile's
hanging down with this warning: "Attention,
Roof Repairs!" Nonetheless
you keep hoping the dove would
fall down into your hand
and ruffle its feathers. Yet more likely
it's a flowerpot, which the cleaning lady
absentmindedly knocks off the ledge, which
kills someone...

You laugh: I've never waited for
a dove, never for the whirring, the falling
of ruffled feathers. I want,
without knowing why,
to run along the houses
with my hand open, even where roofs
are being replaced and snow's sliding
in great chunks and rumbling. Without
knowing why. Because what never, what never
falls down lightly, that's a dove.

PIRATES

The gate's still resisting
at noon. The child's
climbing the wall
and singing. The dogs crawl away
into the rooms. At night
the gate skips open, and someone carries
the dogs, all tied up, to the harbor.
The bushes
will overgrow the courtyard.
The child will wake up under
the leaves, when a caterpillar
crawls over its eyelid.

WAITING 1

Can't you wait till
the grave caves in over you,
why are you knocking, why crying?
Can't you wait till
the ball hits you hard in the chest,
why are you knocking, why crying?
Can't you wait till the child
with the dirty finger strokes
your chin, astonished,
why are you knocking, why crying?
Can't you wait for the humid
spring, for children, for games that
fortuitously set you free, why
are you knocking, why crying?
Can't you wait?

THE FIRE

The first floor's burning.
The children
keep sitting on the carpet and playing.
The fire engine
stops at the house, the spraying
rouses the flames.

The children keep sitting and playing,
although someone shouts at them and puts
up ladders: the bare
trees in the garden resist the sky.
The children don't need
any other salvation.

THE BLACK PAPER

The black paper,
a wind carries it into a ditch along the sidewalk,
into the dust, which
came this way from the excavation:
there was a toy locomotive wrapped
in it. Who can still
grab it out of the ditch,
the dust, which came this way
from the excavation? A wind's
got hold of it, dirty and torn now,
and's carried, taken it away,
the black paper.

THE TRUNK

You can scarcely breathe now. The other
children have left
the attic. You hear your name
from the steps. Something's
pressing hard into your bottom. A dog
died here years ago. Faster
than you. You're still pressing against
the top of the trunk and can
breathe some more. But
your arm is too weak.

In the night you'll still hear someone
coming to fetch the mask of the male gardener, the mask
of the woman gardener too from the cabinet.
But no longer will you
call out, no longer press against the top
of the chest. You'll still hear the rustling,
the tittering. And then,
before you suffocate, the rasping, the rustling,
the tittering coming up from the steps.

MICE

There's just
a tiny little opening
in the gate.
We carry the straws
inside, one by one.
Eventually the grandchildren
will get lost among the heaps
scattered around and choke
to death in the black barn.

INCANTATION

I

But we wanted to make
a ball together
compact reflective
and smooth on the outside so
the rain would run down lightning flashes
bounce off and when it fell
to earth simply rolled
away unharmed.

But inside would be
gardens with fountains with beds
full of roses would be
soft meadows and mountains
blue as of Bassano
and woods above all
woods the under-
growth impenetrable.

Interior wilderness for you
and for me interior refuge
a ball
for you and for me
that's what we wanted to make.

II

Warm and powerful
soft
carried unchecked
outside and without knowing
give yourself surrender yourself
carried outside
and no
coast and no
mountains behind
but the roar the voyage
carried outside
rudderless and without
a wheel give yourself
to the waves and without
knowing being
carried outside
surrender yourself.

III

Counter-
steer against
the current and ever
faster the wake the
crimson swirl and the
ribs of ships and the
burst crates strewn
buried in the mud the
coins of doges the

gurgling cold
counter-
steer against
the lion winged
overpowering.

IV

No stirring
inside you hear
nothing of the turmoil
the noise outside in the
shade of the tree the
stillness for you
inside
stillness for me.

V

Trees the last
at the edge and inside
the thornbush about to
arrive and to
burn up and ashes and at one
with the sand the desire.

But the swamped woods afterward
but
the lament of the birds.

IV

WHO KNOWS?

RIDDLE

Or up there on the
white surface over
the rising water
if now a gust of wind
shredded the clouds the clouds
or the lightning cut up
the swath the lightning
for a moment everything
greatly set agleam for a moment
everything in fog
or up there who knows on the white
surface or over the rising
water who knows?

WAITING 2

Lying motionless in the shallow
motionless water motionless
in the imperceptible
roving sun.
Waiting for the fish with the coin in its belly
for the dove with the news in its beak.
Waiting for the wave that catches for the
wave that carries away.
And lying and waiting.

THE CAT

Running around
in a circle, the cat,
smooth as velvet,
pushes pebbles aside.
They gleam and dazzle, so that
the cat stumbles over the dead
mice, huffy now
because it's kept from running
smooth as velvet in a circle.

TWILIGHT

Twilight and a breeze
from the meadows.
The path
a snake alone
into the unknown and white.

ALLEE

Only a giant is big
enough to hold on to the trunks.
Down below the fireflies
lead you astray, you run
to the fence of the tennis court, a ball's
locked inside. You let yourself down
by the wet rope, sink
through the walkway. It's freezing
in the roar of the jetfighter, except for
the highest treetop, greedily
licking at the dawn.

ON THE DEATH OF
THE ACTOR JAMES DEAN

The poplar in the window's fleeing the curtain,
which spurred on by wind's pursuing it,
while your eye's trying to read the ballet partituras from afar.

Your eye's dispatching the airplane kite,
holding it tight on the leash of its desire,
to drop at one in the morning the droning packet of memory into your sleep.

Nearest your eye, the one
in Cinemascope's dripping the honey of his glance down from the Ferris wheel:

sending it to Paso Robles, in order not to see it anymore.
And rightly so, Achilles always finds his Troy everywhere,
even if they've painted over the slab on the turnpike:

The honey's dripping again into the expressed juice of the grape that won't stop
    growing.
The wreckage of the car's smoking, and it stinks of burned rubber,
so they won't need to build a woodpile anymore.

THE SPANISH STEPS

Only when, frightened by the little dog
that jumped up at my handlebars wound around with flowers,
I'd fallen,
and my bike lay all bent up by the obelisk,
did I, fishes, notice you,
swimming around blind unflinching
in the glassy terraces of the steps
and only heard the women selling flowers complain
about the meager take of the day melting away.

Hence you're still swimming through my brow
when from my room I roam
across the map of the court cartographer Iljin's Russian realm
and when at the foot of the Caucasus' obelisk
my bike lies twisted
and the flower petals are strewn all the way to Finland:
do you swim blind unflinching in the glassy terraces.

ON THE SWING

On the swing the shaggy dog's
looking at me, now from below, now from above, and shaking its hair.
Only when he sees you, blind woman,
you who're sitting veiled on the wall of the fountain,
does he howl loudly on the swing.
But soon again he's looking, now from below, now from above
at me on the swing and shaking his hair.

THE VANISHED ONE

When the fisherman
landed at the foot of the cliff,
climbed up and touched the shoulder of the stranger,
the stranger, who'd long been kneeling, eyes closed,
finally lifted his eye and saw
that having left his native strand full of enemies
and was here now on this distant strand
he had a fisherman for a friend.

na

through ceilings and floors
at the piano the pupil charms it up
it winds around the legs of the old man at the table.

Not till later does he startle,
because he was too busy trying
to refocus his eye, which hung over
the city, cast down in the great storm.

But by now the stringy liana
has wound around his body, his arms,
and won't let him grasp the bits and pieces,
while below the metronome stirs the pupil
insistently softly to the last etude.

DON'T YOU KNOW?

Don't you know the
street the flakes
in the fog
and after slipping through
behind the hedge suddenly
the smell of the wild
don't you know it and behind
the strips of sand and
run aground in the shallow
water the wreck and
without windows and emptied
out and
without doors?

THE CRICKET

Deep in the hollow the cricket sings its song,
too deep, can't catch the wave, which shivers,
reflected from afar over the dome of the hollow.

Too faint the cricket's song in the hollow
and can't catch the wave.

Too deep the cricket
too deep in the hollow and singing,
singing its song
that glows faintly and can't catch the wave, shivering.

FIREFLIES

Sweet scents billowing in clouds from the lilacs,
scents of night and saddening me.
The clouds summon sparks from the lilacs,
saddening me nights,
the fragrant air electrifying the sparks.

Comes a roar to shred the lilacs.
Sweet air billowing nights,
the elephant lying dead in the clouds.
The air's making me sad, setting off sparks.
Dead in the night's sparks,
dead the elephant lying in the lilacs.

WARNING

The bull stands in the entry of the shed
and doesn't enter: he's less afraid
of your bee than the flashing potsherd. Steer
your bee past him to the potsherd!
It won't sting it.
But if it stings the bull,
he'll turn around and drown
your ear in a roar. And you'll never
hear the bull roar again in the entry to the shed.

BALLOON TRIP

The last of the ballast thrown
over and the gorges
blue.
The dizziness.
The sun hot.
Hotter.
Snow-white.

MOON LANDING

Slain in the crater the shepherd.
The flock strangled
in the stony seas. The hatred
insatiable.

WEEDS OF FORGET1

Weeds of forgetting. And then
still a vivid
potsherd in the sand on
the broad shore of forgetting. Fog
over the water and nowhere
another shore.

ACKNOWLEDGMENTS

In memory of Kuno Raeber, and thanks to Bruce, Deborah, and Dennis: three Raeber readers extraordinaire.

Thanks as well to Christiane Wyrwa for valuable suggestions.

This collection would not be possible without the support and many kindnesses of Friederike Barakat and permission to print granted by Carl Hanser Verlag/Munich.

Thanks to the editors of the following journals, in which some of the poems have appeared, sometimes in slightly different form:

American Letters & Commentary, The Aurorean, basalt, Cloudbank, Field, Great River Review, Kestrel, New Delta Review, Notre Dame Review, Pleiades, Plume, Prairie Schooner, Rattle, Red Wheelbarrow, Sou'wester, Time of Singing, The Unrorean

KUNO RAEBER (1922-1992)

THE SWISS WRITER'S considerable body of work—poems, novels, stories, radio and theatrical plays, essays, translations, and reviews—is finally getting the attention it deserves, thanks in large part to a seven-volume edition recently published in Europe (I-V: Carl Hanser Verlag; VI-VII: scaneg Verlag), superbly edited by Christiane Wyrwa & Matthias Klein.

Raeber was a devoted student of theology, philosophy, history, literature, and mythology, who also studied for the priesthood; but as Wyrwa has written, Raeber would soon lose his faith after a deep spiritual crisis, though the images of his religious upbringing never left him. "They were instead transformed into metaphors that blend Christian imagery with a broader mystical tradition to celebrate the power of poetic creation," she went on to note.

In 1958, Raeber began a new life as a freelance writer. An early member of Gruppe 47, at first enduring some some nasty criticism from fellow writers, he spent some anxious years working past "the noise" until emerging as an original in his own right, who lived and wrote by his own lights.

In 1967-68, Raeber was Oberlin College's first Max Kade Writer-in-Residence, replacing Stuart Friebert on sabbatical. The two forged a working relationship that has eventually resulted in this collection, with a companion volume to follow. Raeber would spend considerable time in the U.S., especially in New York, which with Frankfurt, Rome, and Munich became focal locations for most everything else he wrote.

ABOUT THE TRANSLATOR

BORN IN WISCONSIN, Stuart Friebert spent an undergraduate year in Germany as one of the first U.S. exchange students after World War II (1949-50), after which he finished a B.A. (1952) at Wisconsin State College/Milwaukee, and took an M.A. (1953), and a Ph.D. (1957) at U. Wisconsin/Madison in German Language & Literature. He taught at Mt. Holyoke College and Harvard University before settling at Oberlin College in 1961. At Oberlin he taught German, and with colleagues founded Oberlin's Creative Writing Program, which he directed until retiring in 1997. He also co-founded (with David Young) the journal *FIELD,* and later the *FIELD* Translation Series and Oberlin College Press.

He has published twenty-five books of poetry, prose, translations, and with David Young) edited two anthologies. His *Funeral Pie* co-won the Four Way Book Award in 1997. *On the Bottom,* his fourteenth book of poems, is scheduled for publication with Iris Press. Since 2000, he has published a number of stories and memoir-pieces, which are collected in a volume entitled, *The Language of the Enemy,* to be published by Black Mountain Press in 2015. He has also published numerous critical essays and reviews, held an N.E.A. Fellowship in poetry, and received a number of awards for poems and translations over the years.

MORE POETRY FROM TIGER BARK PRESS